JOHN CENA

RAPPING WRESTLER WITH ATTITUDE

by Lucia Raatma

Consultant:
Mike Johnson, Writer
PWInsider.com

CAPSTONE PRESS
a capstone imprint

Velocity is published by Capstone Press,
1710 Roe Crest Drive, North Mankato, Minnesota 56003.
www.capstonepub.com

Library of Congress Cataloging-in-Publication Data
Raatma, Lucia.
    John Cena : rapping wrestler with attitude / by Lucia Raatma.
    p. cm. — (Velocity. pro wrestling stars)
    Includes bibliographical references and index.
    Summary: "Describes the life of John Cena, both in and out of the ring"—Provided
by publisher.
    ISBN 978-1-4296-8676-1 (library binding)
    ISBN 978-1-62065-359-3 (ebook pdf)
    1. Cena, John—Juvenile literature. 2. Wrestlers—United States—Biography—Juvenile
literature. 3. Motion picture actors and actresses—United States—Biography—Juvenile
literature. I. Title.
GV1196.C46R33 2013
796.812092—dc23 [B]   2012011302

Editorial Credits
Mandy Robbins, editor; Sarah Bennett, designer; Laura Manthe, production specialist

Photo Credits
DVIDS/Multi-National Division Baghdad photo by Staff Sgt. Daleanne Maxwell, 4; Getty
Images for KCA: KCA2010/Charley Gallay, 44; Getty Images: Film Magic/George Napolitano,
41 (top), LatinContent/Jam Media/Alfredo Lopez, 38-39, Moses Robinson, 34-35, WireImage
for BWR Public Relations/Photo by J. Shearer, 28, WireImage/Bob Levey, cover, WireImage/
Don Arnold, 32; Globe Photos: John Barrett, 17, 19, 20, 24-25, 26-27; Newscom: Mark
Gordon Company, The Midnight Sun Pictures/WWE Films/Patti Perret/Album, 43, Sipa
Press/Daniel Bersak, 27 (inset), WENN Photos/Carrie Devorah, 14, 37, WENN Photos/
SI1, 9, ZUMA Press, 23, Zuma Press/UPN-TV/WWF, 16; Photo by Wrealano@aol.com, 6,
13, 22 (top); Shutterstock: Andrew Buckin, 30-31 (darts), Andrii Muzyka, 15, Brocreative,
10-11, carroteater, 44 (tv frame), ChromaCo, 11, David Touchstone, 41 (bottom), Gelpi,
33, Georgios Kollidas, 30-31 (dart board), Master3D, 12-13 (road), montego, 8, Nayashkova
Olga, 45, Nejron Photo, 4 (inset flag), Sam Aronov, 31 (Cena), SSylenko, 7; Wikimedia:
Fatima, cover, 1 (background), Randy Chancellor, 22 (bottom)

Artistic Effects
Shutterstock

Printed in the United States of America in Stevens Point, Wisconsin.
032012   006678WZF12

TABLE OF CONTENTS

INTRODUCTION
WRESTLING IN IRAQ

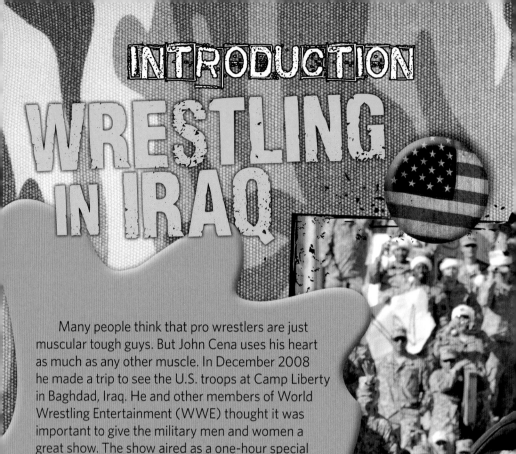

Many people think that pro wrestlers are just muscular tough guys. But John Cena uses his heart as much as any other muscle. In December 2008 he made a trip to see the U.S. troops at Camp Liberty in Baghdad, Iraq. He and other members of World Wrestling Entertainment (WWE) thought it was important to give the military men and women a great show. The show aired as a one-hour special on NBC.

The main event was a six-man **tag team** match. John Cena, Batista, and Rey Mysterio defeated Big Show, Randy Orton, and Chris Jericho. But the visit was about more than just wrestling. John enjoyed talking to the troops and joking with them. John is a rap artist, too, so he performed a holiday song written just for them. It was called "Christmas in Iraq."

This was not John's first trip to Iraq. He had also visited the troops there in 2003. John returned to Baghdad again in 2009. That time he defeated Chris Jericho in a WWE Championship match.

tag team—when two or more wrestlers partner together against other teams

JOHN CENA

HEIGHT
6 feet, 1 inch (185 centimeters)

WEIGHT
251 pounds (114 kilograms)

NICKNAMES
The Prototype
Dr. of Thuganomics
The Marine
The Franchise
Chain Gang Commander
Super Cena

SIGNATURE MOVES
Attitude Adjustment
Pumphandle Slam
Stepover Toehold Facelock

FACT

The WWE has been holding *Tribute to the Troops* since 2003.
WWE wrestlers have visited U.S. military troops in both
Iraq and Afghanistan.

CHAPTER 1
GROWING UP STRONG

Jonathan Felix Anthony Cena was born on April 23, 1977, in West Newbury, Massachusetts. His parents are Carol and John Cena Sr. John's dad loved to watch pro wrestling on TV. In fact, that was the only reason the family had cable TV in their home.

MATT

DAN

FACT

When John was a kid, a couple of his favorite pro wrestlers were Hulk Hogan (right) and André the Giant (left).

JOHN

As a child, John had a collection of wrestling action figures. He built a small wrestling ring for them to fight in. He also made a wrestling championship belt out of paper. John still has that belt today.

SEAN

STEVE

John liked to roughhouse and wrestle with his four brothers, Dan, Matt, Steve, and Sean. They would wrestle outside on the lawn and downstairs in the basement. John liked to pretend he was Hulk Hogan.

JOHN SR.
+
CAROL

Today John Sr. works in the pro wrestling industry. He is known as Johnny Fabulous. Johnny Fabulous is an announcer for Chaotic Wrestling, which is based in North Andover, Massachusetts. He is also the commissioner for East Coast Championship Wrestling.

BULKING UP

When John was young, he was skinny. Other kids picked on him and bullied him. He hated being teased, and he wanted to get strong. When he was 13, John asked his parents to buy him a set of weights. He started working out and has been dedicated to being fit ever since.

STRENGTH TRAINING 101

How does John stay strong? He works out and trains hard. Try some of these exercises if you want to start building muscle like John did:

CORE

(The core includes your back, hips, and stomach muscles.)

Plank: Lie facedown on a mat. Keep your lower arms on the mat, and lift up your chest so your elbows are at 90-degree angles. Lift your lower half up onto your toes. Keep your body straight and your stomach muscles tight. If your back start sagging, tighten your stomach muscles. Hold this position as long as possible.

TIP

When choosing hand weights, don't overdo the weight. Strengthen your muscles by repeating the exercise instead of straining muscles with weights that are too heavy for you.

ARMS

Standing curl: Grasp hand weights with an underhand grip. Keep your arms facing forward and elbows to the side. Bend at the elbows and raise the weights until the forearms are vertical. Lower the arms until they are extended.

SHOULDERS

Standing shoulder press: Stand with your feet shoulder-width apart. Grasp the ends of a resistance band in each hand with your palms facing down. Stand on the band to create tension. Raise your hands overhead and extend your arms. Lower your hands to your nose and repeat.

LEGS

Lunges: Face forward and stand with your feet hip-width apart. Take a big step forward with your right foot. Bend your knee and lower your body until your thigh is **parallel** with the floor. Make sure your knee lines up with your ankle. Push off the floor with your right foot. Return to a standing position. Repeat the exercise with your left foot and leg.

parallel—an equal distance apart; parallel lines never cross or meet

9

CHAPTER 2
ONE TOUGH COMPETITOR

Working out helped John become a great athlete. He went to high school at Cushing Academy in Ashburnham, Massachusetts. John played on the football team and loved it.

John chose to attend Springfield College in Massachusetts, where he was a star on the football team. He played center, which is a position on the offensive line. John was the first person at practice and often the last one to leave. In fact, during his college days, John never missed a football practice or a game. He was known for motivating the team and giving pep talks to the other players. John was the team captain during his senior year. He was also named an All-American player.

FACT

While in college, John watched WWE's *Raw* on Monday nights.

John played hard in college, but he studied hard too. He majored in **physiology**. John continued to do bodybuilding, and he hoped to one day be a personal trainer.

physiology—the study of how the body works

THE ROAD TO PRO WRESTLING

After college, John moved to southern California. He worked in a gym, coaching other people in their workouts. At the gym John met a man who was training to become a pro wrestler. John had always loved pro wrestling, and the idea of becoming a pro wrestler appealed to him. John enrolled in a pro wrestling training school called Ultimate University. A group called Ultimate Pro Wrestling (UPW) ran this school.

Soon John was competing in the UPW. The UPW was a small operation, and he didn't make much money. But John was gaining a lot of wrestling experience.

Jim Ross was a **scout** for the WWE. He flew to California to see John in action. Ross signed John to a contract with the WWE. But first John had to compete in Ohio Valley Wrestling (OVW). That was a training program for the WWE.

Randy Orton was an up-and-coming wrestler who John met in OVW. Randy and John often competed against each other in OVW. Though they were rivals in the ring, they became great friends outside the ring.

scout—a person who works for an athletic organization looking for new talent

While John was in the OVW, he met another wrestler named **Batista**. Batista had won the OVW Championship but then lost it to Cena.

As chairman of WWE, **Vince McMahon** was interested to see what kind of talent his new wrestlers had. John wanted to prove himself to McMahon. He told McMahon that he would one day headline *WrestleMania*.

CHAPTER 3

A WRESTLER WITH ATTITUDE

Every wrestler has a **gimmick**. Some have crazy hairdos, and some wear wacky costumes. Fans love gimmicks. They help make each wrestler unique.

John's gimmick came naturally. He had always loved hip-hop music, and he enjoyed doing **freestyle rap**. John used to entertain his fellow wrestlers by rapping before matches. As his professional career grew, John took on the image of an all-American rap singer. He used rhyming to tease and taunt his competitors.

In 2003, after a televised WWE competition called *Vengeance*, John was ready to take on Orlando Jordan. But John was also feuding with Undertaker at that time. Before his match with Jordan, John let Undertaker know he hadn't forgotten about their feud. Check out part of the rap he performed before his match with Jordan:

You see, at *Vengeance*, everybody
saw that Cena failed the test.
But it was Undertaker who
left the arena a bloody mess!

Yeah yeah yeah, he's sitting at home,
I'm standing here, okay?
And I'm demanding a rematch
on *SmackDown* next Thursday!

He's a big coward,
and I guarantee he's a no show.
He's too busy hitting on those rookies,
trying to get a low blow.

gimmick—a clever trick or idea used to get people's attention

freestyle rap—the type of rap that a person makes up on the spot

JOHN CENA VS. KURT ANGLE

John made his WWE **debut** on June 27, 2002, against Kurt Angle. The match-up was broadcast on *SmackDown*. John showed some promise when he managed to kick out of the Angle Slam, one of Angle's toughest moves. But he didn't win the match. Even though John lost, fans saw that he was tough.

John was not discouraged by his first loss. A few weeks later, on July 11, he got revenge. John teamed up with Undertaker. Together they defeated the team of Kurt Angle and Chris Jericho. It was John's first taste of victory in the WWE.

KURT ANGLE

HEIGHT
6 ft (183 cm)

WEIGHT
240 lbs (109 kg)

NICKNAMES
The American Hero
The Wrestling Machine

SIGNATURE MOVES
Angle Slam Bodyscissors
Double Leg Takedown

debut—someone's first public appearance

JOHN CENA VS. BROCK LESNAR

In early 2003 John set his sights on the WWE Championship. He challenged champ Brock Lesnar to wrestle him for the title. Lesnar refused and ignored all of Cena's taunts. But in April 2003 John entered a tournament in which the winner would earn the right to fight Lesnar. John defeated Chris Benoit to win that right.

John was excited to take on Lesnar, and he fought hard. But the champ proved too much for him. Lesnar beat John and kept his title. No matter how disappointed he was, though, John shook off the defeat. He said he was not afraid to fail, and he would just keep trying.

BROCK LESNAR

HEIGHT
6 ft, 3 in (190.5 cm)

WEIGHT
280 lbs (127 kg)

NICKNAME
The Next Big Thing

SIGNATURE MOVES
Backbreaker
Fallaway Slam

17

CHAPTER 4

BECOMING A CHAMPION

Imagine a match that involves 30 wrestlers! That's the scene of WWE's *Royal Rumble*. Each wrestler is given a number, and the match begins with wrestlers number one and number two facing off. The remaining wrestlers enter the ring every few minutes, depending on their numbers. Wrestlers are eliminated when they are thrown over the ropes. The last man standing wins.

John entered the *Royal Rumble* in January 2004. He gave it a good effort and made it to the last six wrestlers. But the reigning WWE U.S. Champion, Big Show, eliminated him.

COUNT THOSE TITLES!

Through 2011, here is how John Cena and Big Show matched up:

John Cena ⭐
Big Show ⭐

	WWE U.S. Champ	WWE Champ	WWE Tag Team Champ	World Tag Team Champ	World Heavyweight Champ
John Cena	3	10	2	2	2
Big Show	1	2	3	5	1

Two months later, John was ready to take on Big Show again. They met at *WrestleMania* in New York City's Madison Square Garden. John didn't let his huge opponent intimidate him. He attacked Big Show and finally slammed him to the mat. John had won his first U.S. championship!

STAYING ON TOP

One of the difficult things about being a WWE U.S. Champion is holding on to the title. John experienced the roller coaster ride of being a champ in 2004.

MARCH 14, 2004
John won his first WWE U.S. Championship at *WrestleMania*.

JULY 6, 2004
John lost his title when he was accused of a rules violation. The accusation came from Kurt Angle, who was the *SmackDown* general manager.

NOVEMBER 16, 2004
John defeated Carlito to win the championship again.

OCTOBER 3, 2004
John defeated Booker T to regain the title. This match-up was the fifth match in a grueling best-of-five series.

OCTOBER 5, 2004
Just two days after beating Booker T, John lost the title to Carlito Caribbean Cool.

WHAT DO THOSE TITLES MEAN?

The WWE has many different championship titles. They are separated between the *Raw* and *SmackDown* brands, which are two different TV programs. Check out the main titles:

RAW

The WWE Championship is the primary title for the *Raw* brand. It was established in 1963.

The U.S. Championship is the secondary title for the *Raw* brand. It was first created in 1975 by the National Wrestling Alliance (NWA).

SMACKDOWN

The World Heavyweight Championship is the primary title for the *SmackDown* brand. It was started in 2002.

The Intercontinental Championship is the second most important title for the *SmackDown* brand. It started in 1979.

CHAPTER 5

SIGNATURE CENA

Like other pro wrestlers, John has signature moves that he is known for. Opponents dread them, and fans look forward to seeing them.

John often taunts his opponents just before laying down a signature move. One of his most famous taunts is called "You Can't See Me." John waves his hand in front of his face and says, "You can't see me!"

JOHN'S FAVORITE SIGNATURE MOVES

Other than taunting his opponents, John also lays down his favorite moves. Check out some of John's signature moves:

FIVE KNUCKLE SHUFFLE

This move starts when an opponent is already down on the mat. John starts it with the You Can't See Me, and follows up with a falling punch to the shoulder.

STEPOVER TOEHOLD FACELOCK (STF)

When an opponent is facedown, John lies on top of him, grabs the other wrestler's ankle, and places it between his thighs. Then he wraps his arms around the other wrestler's head and pulls it back.

ATTITUDE ADJUSTMENT

John lifts up his opponent and then falls forward, slamming the other wrestler's back to the mat.

PUMPHANDLE SLAM

This is a variation of the Attitude Adjustment. John lifts his opponent up in the air and places him on his shoulder, facedown. Then he slams his opponent's back on the mat and pins him down.

SIGNATURE OBJECTS

As part of his rapper gimmick, John dresses the part. He often wears knee-length jean shorts and pump-up sneakers. Here are other items he is known for.

BASEBALL CAP

Like many rap artists, John usually wears a baseball cap. He often wears it backward.

CHAIN PENDANT

John wears a thick chain and pendant around his neck. His fans often call themselves the Chain Gang. John's pendant was once a lock. He replaced it with a spinning Chain Gang medallion.

BRASS KNUCKLES

This weapon is one piece that fits around all four knuckles. It's usually made of steel, not brass.

SPORTS JERSEY

John likes to wear sports jerseys that represent the cities he competes in. He sometimes wears number 54. It was the number he wore as a college football player.

DOG TAGS (not shown)

John has great respect for the U.S. military. To show this respect, he sometimes wears dog tags. Soldiers wear these metal IDs on chains around their necks.

FACT

As another way to show his respect for the military, John wears T-shirts or caps with a camouflage pattern.

JOHN'S U.S. CHAMPIONSHIP BELT

After winning the WWE U.S. Championship in 2004, John wanted to have a custom-made championship belt. John's belt symbolized his love for wrestling, hip-hop, and the United States.

SPINNING CENTER PLATE

It is similar to spinning center plates that are used as decorations inside car wheels. These are often popular with hip-hop fans.

WORDS

Two big block letters—"U.S."—are shown in white. Above the letters is the phrase "Word Life," which is the title of one of John's rap songs. Below the block letters is his name.

FLAGS AND STARS

The patriotic theme continues with images of U.S. flags and stars on both sides.

COLORS

The spinning plate had a red, white, and blue American flag background.

FACT

John lost his custom belt in a match against Orlando Jordan on March 3, 2005. Jordan destroyed the belt and replaced it with the original WWE U.S. Championship belt.

John's custom belt, worn by a ball girl for his favorite baseball team

NOT A QUITTER

After winning the U.S. Championship, John had his sights set on the WWE Championship. He got his shot at the title during a *WrestleMania* fight in April 2005. John faced John Bradshaw Layfield (JBL). It was a tough match. John had to escape a number of **submission holds**. In the end, he pinned JBL and claimed the WWE Championship.

JOHN BRADSHAW LAYFIELD

HEIGHT
6 ft, 6 in (198 cm)

WEIGHT
290 lbs (132 kg)

NICKNAMES
JBL

SIGNATURE MOVES
Clothesline from Hell

submission hold—a chokehold, joint hold, or compression lock that causes a fighter's opponent to end the match by tapping out or saying, "I submit"

It wasn't long before JBL challenged John for the title again. In May 2005, the two met at a *Judgment Day* showdown. They were set to fight an "I Quit" match. This meant they would continue to fight until one of them yelled, "I quit!"

And what a show it was! JBL entered the arena in a limousine. John rode in on the back of a semi truck that shot fireworks into the air.

The two men slammed each other onto the mat. JBL smashed John with a chair and tried to choke him with a cord. The fight moved to the limousine, and John punched JBL's head through a window. Then John tore an exhaust pipe from the truck and ran toward JBL, shoving him toward a wall. "I quit!" JBL yelled. And John remained the WWE Champion.

FACT

After John won the WWE Championship, he had another custom belt created. It featured a gold and diamond design with a spinning WWE logo in the center.

COUNT THOSE TITLES!

Through 2011, here is how John Cena and JBL matched up:

John Cena
JBL

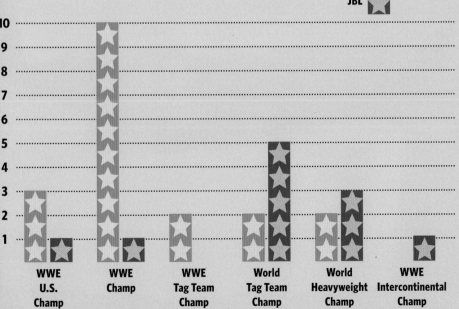

CHAPTER 6

FAMOUS FEUDS

Over the years, John has had some heated rivalries with other wrestlers. These opponents would love to use John's face as a dartboard.

JBL

Height: 6 ft, 6 in (198 cm)

Weight: 290 lbs (132 kg)

JBL and John feuded for the WWE Championship in 2005.

EDGE

Height: 6 ft, 5 in (196 cm)

Weight: 241 lbs (109 kg)

Edge has faced off with John many times. He once even interfered with a match to help Rob Van Dam defeat John.

THE MIZ

Height: 6 ft, 1 in (185 cm)

Weight: 231 lbs (105 kg)

The Miz and John have challenged each other to matches over the years. They worked together as a tag team for one match, but that partnership didn't last. In May 2011, John defeated The Miz in a Triple Cage Match.

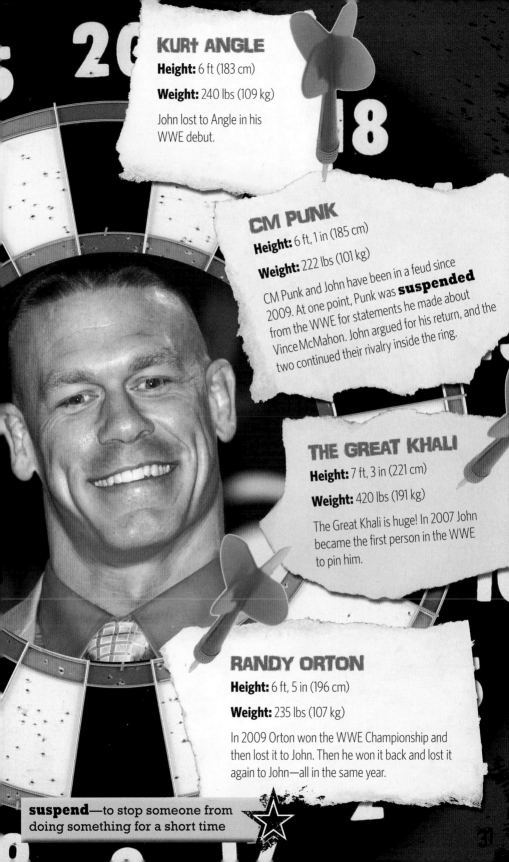

KURT ANGLE

Height: 6 ft (183 cm)

Weight: 240 lbs (109 kg)

John lost to Angle in his WWE debut.

CM PUNK

Height: 6 ft, 1 in (185 cm)

Weight: 222 lbs (101 kg)

CM Punk and John have been in a feud since 2009. At one point, Punk was **suspended** from the WWE for statements he made about Vince McMahon. John argued for his return, and the two continued their rivalry inside the ring.

THE GREAT KHALI

Height: 7 ft, 3 in (221 cm)

Weight: 420 lbs (191 kg)

The Great Khali is huge! In 2007 John became the first person in the WWE to pin him.

RANDY ORTON

Height: 6 ft, 5 in (196 cm)

Weight: 235 lbs (107 kg)

In 2009 Orton won the WWE Championship and then lost it to John. Then he won it back and lost it again to John—all in the same year.

ON THE EDGE

Throughout 2006, John and Edge came at each other over and over again. John was the WWE Champion as the year began, but Edge earned the title on January 8. Then John won it back on January 29.

John and Edge faced off at the WWE *Raw Superslam* event on August 4, 2006.

EDGE

HEIGHT
6 ft, 5 in (196 cm)

WEIGHT
241 lbs (109 kg)

NICKNAMES
Rated "R" Superstar

SIGNATURE MOVES
Spear

On September 17, 2006, John and Edge faced each other again. This was a Tables, Ladders, and Chairs (TLC) match. They could use both tables and chairs to fight each other. The WWE Championship belt was hung above the ring. Whichever wrestler could set up the ladder and climb to the top to reach the belt first would be named the champion.

The match was action-packed. John and Edge traded blows, whacking each other with chairs and slamming each other into tables. After brutal exchanges, they both were climbing the ladder and they both reached the top. John grabbed Edge, lifted him up, and tossed him onto two tables stacked next to the ladder. John grabbed the championship belt. The WWE Champion title was his once again!

COUNT THOSE TITLES!

Through 2011, here is how John Cena and Edge matched up:

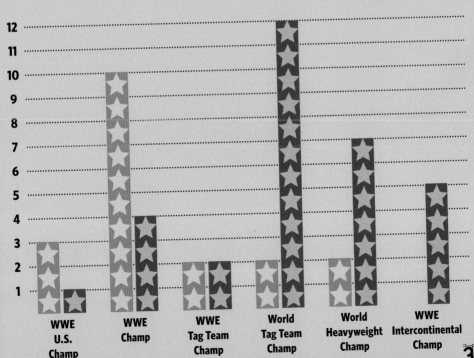

John Cena
Edge

CHAPTER 7

A BIG MAN WITH BIG NAMES

John is known best by his real name. But over the years, he has had a number of nicknames.

THE PROTOTYPE

This was John's first professional name, which he used in UPW. A prototype is an early model of something that people try to copy. His look at the time was supposed to be part man, part machine. He sported bleach-blond hair and was meant to look like the peak of physical perfection.

THE FRANCHISE

A franchise is a business that uses the model of a larger business as a guide. John has been a big part of the WWE business. He and the WWE have made a lot of money because he follows the guidelines of the big organization.

SUPER CENA

This nickname is a play on "Superman." Sometimes John does seem superhuman!

CHAIN GANG COMMANDER

Because of the large chain John often wears, fans call themselves the Chain Gang. So naturally, John is the Chain Gang Commander.

THE MARINE

With his buzz-cut hair, John has the look of a pumped-up military man. He also made a movie about a marine and has a strong respect for people who serve in the military.

DR. OF THUGANOMICS

John has often joked that he has a degree in "thuganomics." A "thug" is another term for a tough guy. This word is commonly used in rap culture. And "anomics" is often added to the end of a word to mean the study of something. John wanted people to know that no one was tougher than he was.

FACT

Pro Wrestling Illustrated named John Wrestler of the Year in 2006 and 2007.

THE BIGGER T
THE HARDER T

Pro wrestling can be hard on the body. John has suffered a number of injuries during his career. Some have kept him out of action for a few days. Others have required weeks or months to recover.

HEAD INJURY

All athletes run the risk of getting **concussions**. With all the body slams, wrestlers often suffer many concussions. A concussion should fully heal before an athlete is active again. If an athlete gets another head injury before the concussion heals, he could have permanent brain damage. In 2011 John reportedly suffered a concussion, but some people questioned whether the injury was real. In any case, he was back in the ring within two weeks.

NECK INJURY

With all the holds that wrestlers force on one another, it's no wonder that wrestlers' necks get hurt. In 2008 John had a **herniated disk** in his neck that required surgery. It took him several months to recover.

RIGHT HIP INJURY

In December 2010 John suffered a deep bruise to his hip during a match. He was worried that it was very serious, but he healed quickly. John was back in action just a few weeks later.

TORN RIGHT PECTORAL MUSCLE

2007 John suffered a torn pectoral muscle. The pectoral muscle is the big muscle at the ont of the chest. A tear happens when the **tendon** that connects the muscle to the m is damaged. This injury usually requires surgery. After John had surgery, he worked at s **rehabilitation** for eight hours a day. He was back in the ring four months later.

concussion—an injury to the brain caused by a hard blow to the head

herniated disk—when a spinal disk pops out of place

tendon—a strong band of tissue that attaches muscles to bones

rehabilitation—therapy that helps people recover their health or abilities

Sometimes wrestlers don't fight one-on-one. Instead, they face off in teams—tag teams. John has participated in many tag teams over the years. Here are some of the competitors he has joined forces with.

SHAWN MICHAELS

In January 2007, John Cena and Shawn Michaels took on Randy Orton and Edge. John and Shawn were a tough team to beat. They won the World Tag Team Championship and defended their title against other duos.

John teamed up with Randy Orton for a fight against Sheamus and Batista on May 5, 2010.

BATISTA

In 2008 John teamed up with Batista to take the World Tag Team Championship. They defeated Cody Rhodes and Ted DiBiase Jr.

DAVID OTUNGA

On October 24, 2010, John teamed up with David Otunga to win the WWE Tag Team Championship. They defeated Cody Rhodes and Drew McIntyre. The very next night, they lost the championship to Justin Gabriel and Heath Slater.

THE MIZ

On February 21, 2011, John and The Miz took on Heath Slater and Justin Gabriel. John and The Miz defeated Slater and Gabriel to win the WWE Tag Team Championship. However, they lost the title the same day in a rematch.

CHAPTER 9

OUTSIDE THE RING

MUSIC MAN

When John isn't wrestling, he has a second career as a rap and hip-hop musician. His first album, *You Can't See Me*, was released in 2005. He recorded it with his cousin Tha Trademarc. The album debuted at #15 on the *Billboard 200* chart. One of the singles on the album is "The Time Is Now." John co-wrote this song and he uses it as his wrestling entrance theme. Check out the chorus:

Your time is up, my time is now

You can't see me, my time is now

It's the Franchise, boy I'm shinin' now

You can't see me, my time is now!

MUSCLE MAN

Aside from music and wrestling, John has another love—muscle cars. Muscle cars have engines that are changed to be big and powerful. John's interest in cars goes back to when he was a teenager. He would work on cars in his yard. Today he has a whole collection of muscle cars which he has worked on himself.

In 2011 John met with kids through the Garden of Dreams Foundation. This organization grants wishes to kids facing physical, mental, and emotional challenges.

MAKING WISHES COME TRUE

The Make-A-Wish Foundation grants wishes for children with life-threatening illnesses. Sometimes these kids ask to meet a famous actor or athlete. John has been happy to donate his time to this cause. During his career, he has granted more than 200 wishes to kids.

ON THE SILVER SCREEN

John has shown his talents in movies as well. Take a sneak peek at some of his exciting roles.

THE MARINE

In 2006 John starred in *The Marine*. In this action film, John played John Triton, a marine who has to rescue his kidnapped wife. John's single "If It All Ended Tomorrow" is heard during the final credits for *The Marine*.

LEGENDARY

In this 2010 drama, John played Mike Chetley, a former high school wrestler. In the movie he trains his younger brother, Cal, when Cal decides to join the high school wrestling team.

THE REUNION

In this 2011 drama, a woman tries to bring her brothers back together after their father had died. John played Sam Cleary, one of the brothers, who was a recently suspended police officer.

FACT

John has appeared in TV movies too. He played Fred's imaginary dad in *Fred: The Movie* and *Fred: The Movie 2*. He also appeared in *Inside Wrestling School*, a film about what it's like to train to be a pro wrestler.

12 ROUNDS

This action film hit the screens in 2009. In it John starred as detective Danny Fisher. He had to complete 12 challenges to save his girlfriend.

FAMOUS FACE

Throughout his career, John has become a well-known face on TV. In addition to starring in WWE events, he has appeared on many TV shows. These programs include guest roles on *Hannah Montana, Psych,* and *True Jackson, VP.* John has made appearances on *Jimmy Kimmel Live* and *Late Night with Conan O'Brien.* He and his childhood role model, Hulk Hogan, were presenters at the *2005 Teen Choice Awards.* He and other wrestlers also appeared on an episode of *Extreme Makeover: Home Edition.* In 2008 John appeared with Triple H and Chris Jericho on the *Idol Gives Back* fund-raising special.

John pre-taped an outdoor segment for the *2010 Nickelodeon Kids' Choice Awards* as one of his appearances on the show.

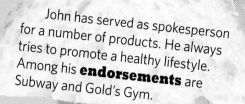

John has served as spokesperson for a number of products. He always tries to promote a healthy lifestyle. Among his **endorsements** are Subway and Gold's Gym.

WHERE WILL JOHN GO FROM HERE?

John takes good care of himself and trains hard. If he can avoid injuries, he may be a pro wrestling champ for many more years. He will likely continue to fight in the ring, act, sing, and make kids' wishes come true.

endorsement—a relationship in which someone sponsors a product by appearing in advertisements or on the product

GLOSSARY

concussion (kuhn-KUH-shuhn)—an injury to the brain caused by a hard blow to the head

debut (day-BYOO)—a first public appearance

endorsement (in-DORS-muhnt)—a relationship in which someone sponsors a product by appearing in advertisements or on the product

freestyle rap (FREE-styl RAP)—a type of rap that a person makes up on the spot

gimmick (GIM-ik)—a clever trick or idea used to get attention

herniated disk (HURN-ee-ay-tud DISK)—an injury that occurs when a spinal disk pops out of place

parallel (PA-ruh-lel)—if two straight lines are parallel, they stay the same distance from each other, and they never cross or meet

physiology (fiz-ee-OL-uh-jee)—the study of how the body works

rehabilitation (ree-huh-bil-uh-TAY-shun)—therapy that helps people recover their health or abilities

scout (SKOUT)—a person who works for an athletic organization looking for new talent

submission hold (sub-MISH-uhn HOLD)—a chokehold, joint hold, or compression lock that causes a fighter's opponent to end the match by tapping out or saying, "I submit"

suspend (suh-SPEND)—to stop someone from doing something for a short time

tag team (TAG TEEM)—two or more wrestlers who partner together against other teams

tendon (TEN-duhn)—a strong band of tissue that attaches muscles to bones

READ MORE

Fandel, Jennifer. *CM Punk: Straight Edge Heel.* Pro Wrestling Stars. North Mankato, Minn.: Capstone Press, 2012.

Grayson, Robert. *John Cena.* Modern Role Models. Philadelphia, Pa.: Mason Crest Publishers, 2009.

O'Shei, Tim. *John Cena.* Stars of Pro Wrestling. Mankato, Minn.: Capstone Press, 2010.

INTERNET SITES

FactHound offers a safe, fun way to find Internet sites related to this book. All of the sites on FactHound have been researched by our staff.

Here's all you do:

Visit *www.facthound.com*

Enter this code: 9781429686761

INDEX